L.

Share your memories with family & friends, turn your memoirs into your book

THE STORY HAS A SECRET

THE STORY HAS A SECRET

Robert D. Brehm

ISBN: 1983897469
ISBN-13: 9781983897467
Library of Congress Control Number: 2018900992
CreateSpace Independent Publishing Platform
North Charleston, South Carolina

CONTENTS

From the Harvard Years

From the University Years

From the Green River Years

PREFACE

ROBERT D. BREHM's therapeutic autobiography is unique in that the author uses his own life as an example.

He intends to provide readers with an autobiography through the author's self-disclosure and with psychological concepts embedded within the stories.

Each story has a secret how the author's stories magically brought him self-awareness. Psychodramatic therapeutic elements such as the "empty chair" and "dialogue" enable the author to re-enact stories in the present time.

Robert D. Brehm demonstrates how the therapeutic autobiographical stories told, or written, offer many therapeutic benefits to the storyteller; serving as a review of one's life purpose and in encouraging introspection that can lead the storyteller to a more fulfilled life.

He invites you to share your story with others. We are the stories we share. Stories focus on the memories of our lives. They become memoires that affirm meaning and involve our families in providing us a strengthened connection.

PART I

THE BOOK IS divided into two parts.

Chapter 1 represents the effect of a car accident on a child. The author re-enacts the situation in the present time and illustrates the insight that he obtained.

Chapters 2-5 depict the dramatic events that happened to him at age four beginning with the farm and ending with the influence on him during World War II. The re-enactment with the "dialogue and empty chair" illustrate its therapeutic use.

Chapters 6-13 represent the religious influence of his living in rural America, the fear associated with discrimination against immigrants, and how the elderly were often housed in insane asylums.

Chapters 14-19 depict the Vietnam war years (1961-1967) that provided impetus for the author to become an educator and therapist.

PART II

THE FOLLOWING STORIES challenge the reader to infer which elements in the story represent the storyteller. The author includes stories (Chapter 20-30) of some of the students who contributed to the motivation for the author's writing the therapeutic autobiography.

Rick (Chapter 21) overcame physical and emotional obstacles to become a successful practicing therapist.

Jack (Chapter 22) overcame the culture of the sixties and became one of the most outstanding prison officials in the country.

Mary (Chapter 23) fulfilled her dream of creating a service agency for adolescents.

Jerry (Chapter 24) lived with his life-long challenges that motivated the author to write this book.

George (Chapter 25) overcame his disability and was able to lead a normal life working as a custodian in a school system.

José (Chapter 26) won his case against race discrimination.

William (Chapter 27) overcame challenges, completed his college education, and became a minister.

Tom (Chapter 28) overcame obstacles and became a very successful Episcopal priest.

Dan (Chapter 29) graduated from the university and became a professional basketball player.

As so what is the rest of the story? (Chapter 30) introduces the reader to the author's intended sequel.

CHAPTER 1

MAN, DON'T YOU EVER DO THAT AGAIN

You are happy to be alive.

MUD SPLASHED IN my eyes. I couldn't see anything. Where was I? I hear voices from above.

"Where is he?"

My mom echoed. "Where is he? Is he okay?"

Someone picked me up and I stuttered, "Man, don't you ever do that again!"

What happened? Someone crashed into us and the force catapulted me out of the car. I landed in a ditch and I was covered with mud.

And it happened so quickly that I did not have time to be afraid. Were I to meet that driver today, I would thank him for teaching me a lesson. As a child I certainly was not aware of attributional errors.[1] Attributional errors are the perceptual errors in assigning responsibility to others or to situations.

A dispositional error blames a person. A situational error blames a situation. Let me give an example with the following.

I stuttered to the driver, "Man, don't you ever do that again."

I committed a dispositional error. I blamed the man.

"I am sorry. This was an accident."

The man committed a situational error. He blamed the situation.

Let me illustrate the how I might role play the scenario today without committing a dispositional or a situational error. I use the empty chair technique.

The empty chair technique, developed by Fritz Perl and J. L. Moreno,[2] is a projection technique designed to assist us in experiencing how we attribute our own characteristics to a person or object.[3]

1 .Don Hamachek, Encounters with Others, New York: Holt, Reinhart & Winston, 1982, p.26

2 Marvin G. Knittel, "Empty Chair Grief Work from a Psychodrama Perspective," *Counseling Today* 52, no. 10 (2010): 50–1.

3 Adam Blather, *Acting-In: Practical Applications of Psychodramatic Methods* (New York: Springer, 1973), 45.

Look at the following example.

I sit on Chair Number 1.

I say to the driver who I imagine is sitting on Chair Number 2.

"Man, don't you ever do that again."

Chair Number 1   Chair Number 2

Now I reverse roles and I sit on Chair Number 2. I assume the position of the driver. I speak to my imaginary self seated upon Chair Number 1.

"Yes, I will be more careful the next time I am driving."

Finally, I reverse roles.

I place myself on Chair Number 1. I speak to Chair Number 2. I imagine the driver sitting on Chair Number 2.

"Thanks. I learned that I am quite capable of handling the situation. I can fly through the air unscathed; however, the next time I will try to land on my feet and not on my face."

In this role-reversal exercise, I took the position of the stranger as I projected him to be, and then I ascribed my own projection to myself by sitting in the empty chair and speaking to myself.

By owning my own projection, I discovered that I was happy to be alive and that I was quite capable of handling the situation.

CHAPTER 2

WHAT A TURKEY TAUGHT ME ABOUT GOBBLEDYGOOK

I WAS BORN on a Nebraska farm and I learned some lessons from the animals. When I think of how many times I have been accused of gobbledygook, I think of Tom the Turkey.

I had been playing outside in the farmyard when Tom the Turkey came right up to me and looked me in the eye. He was about my height and he gobbled and gobbled at me. I ran as fast as I could to the house. I was in tears.

"Dad," I shouted, "Tom the Turkey just about pecked me in the eyes."

Dad looked straight at me and said, "Go back and look him in the eye. Don't ever let any turkey bother you again."

I was scared, but I did trust that I could deal with Tom the Turkey. I walked outside and found Tom the Turkey exactly where he'd been.

I looked him straight in the eyes and said, "Tom the Turkey, don't you ever scare me again." He looked at me a bit and then turned and walked away.

We are not only storytellers, but we also commit attribution errors in sharing our stories. These perceptual errors are particularly noticeable when we use abstract nouns.

Abstract nouns, such as *trust*, exist only in the mind and, by definition, do not exist in situations or in other people.[4] I am reminded of an aphorism.

"Trust thyself only, and another shall not betray thee." -- Thomas Fuller

As a child, I did not realize the word *trust* was an abstract noun and only resided in the eyes of (me) the beholder.[5] I assumed I could not *trust* Tom the Turkey as I ascribed my *distrust* to him.

---

4 "Abstract Noun," *Cambridge Dictionary*, accessed January 20, 2018, http://dictionary.cambridge.org/us/dictionary/english/abstract-noun.

5 "Can You Imagine Being in My Shoes?," Robert Brehm, Stress Guru, accessed January 20, 2018, http://stressguru.com/Interpersonal_Relations/class_16.htm.

Although I followed my dad's instructions at the time, I did not realize the abstract word *trust* resided in my own mind. I projected my *distrust* on Tom the Turkey. I *distrusted* myself, and I assumed I did not have the resources to protect myself from getting hurt, so I committed the dispositional error.

I would place my imaginary Tom the Turkey on Chair Number 1.

I would say:

Tom the Turkey   Me
Chair Number 1   Chair Number 2

"Tom the Turkey, I know you are just looking at me."
I should ask myself the question as I place myself on Chair Number 2.

"Robert, why are you looking at Tom the Turkey wondering why he is looking at you?"

Next, I would speak to Tom the Turkey who I imagine is placed on Chair Number 1.

"Tom the Turkey, I will look at you, and you can look at me if you wish."

Again, I speak to Chair Number 2 taking the position of Tom the Turkey who I imagine is sitting on Chair Number 1.

"Robert, you are looking at me and I am looking at you. I think I now will look at something else."

Finally, taking my position of sitting on Chair Number 2, I reply to my imagined Tom the Turkey who is placed on Chair Number 1.

"Thanks, Tom the Turkey, for the lesson I learned today as I comprehend how abstract words, such as *trust*, exist only in the eye of the   beholder.

"You may be both a concrete and an abstract noun. You are a concrete noun when you exist according to information that I have received from my senses.

"When I imagine your position on the empty chair, however, then I am aware of your existence as an abstract noun.

"I can see how such a distinction might seem like gobbledygook to you, Tom the Turkey, but the distinction between concrete and abstract nouns is now very clear to me."

CHAPTER 3

WILL THE CHICKENS COME HOME TO ROOST?

My DAD WAS a poultry dealer in Harvard, Nebraska. I enjoyed riding with my dad in his 1942 Chevrolet truck visiting the different farms. I was never bored, as I was always trying to help my dad candle chicken eggs. I became quite familiar with his poultry route and how he would candle eggs.[6]

---

6 https://www.wikihow.com/Candle-an-Egg

When I would try to candle the egg, I would hold it up to a bright light to see if there was any embryo in the egg. If any embryo was visible, then I would not select the egg. Dad sold the candled eggs to the Harvard Air Force Base. He sold the chickens to a poultry processing plant.[7] (Can you imagine what occurs there?)

The Harvard Army Air Force Base had an enduring effect on me. I was aware that the Base was important to our training bomber pilots during World War II. And the Base was located only two miles from our home.

I could hear the constant noise from the planes taking off and landing.

Had I known of the rumor that Jimmy Doolittle (Group 17) touched down on its runway in preparation for bombing Japan, the loudest sound would have come from my heart beating in my ear.

The influence was more obvious, however, as the Army housed two couples and a single person in my parent's home with my three sisters and me.

I remember one couple who stayed with us in our home. The wife, named Angel, decided to put her two white mice on the kitchen table and feed them milk out of an eyedropper.

I did not like sharing our dinner table with the two mice and the ten people who were living with us in our

---

7 "Poultry Processing," Joe M. Regenstein and R. Paul Singh, *Encyclopedia Britannica*, accessed January 20, 2018, https://www.britannica.com/topic/poultry-processing.

five-bedroom house. I was happy to leave home every time I could go with my dad on his poultry route.

One very hot summer day on September 15, 1944, I was riding with my dad in his black Chevrolet truck. He was driving on a gravel road near the southern perimeter of the Hastings Naval Ammunition Depot. *Kaboom! Bam!* Smoke belched in the sky. I thought a gust of wind nearly blew off my head!

"Dad, what was that?" I screamed as I saw the huge ball of billowing smoke.

Dad said calmly, "A bomb exploded."[8]

Later that day we learned that the bomb explosion burst many windows in the houses in Harvard. Even the schoolhouse had extensive damage as evidenced by cracked walls. It was not until many years later, however, that I learned that the explosion also killed employees at the Hastings Naval Ammunition Depot.[9]

Had I known more about the war with Germany, I might have been even more frightened with the bomb explosion. Today, I understand how the war heightened anxiety among the German immigrants.

For example, Conrad Brehm, my paternal grandfather, was a German who had immigrated to America from

---

8 "Maker Monday: Harvard Army Air Field," Nebraska State Historical Society, December 5, 2016, https://history.nebraska.gov/blog/marker-monday-harvard-army-air-field.

9 "Hastings Naval Ammunition Depot, Nebraska," Wikipedia, last edited October 24, 2017, https://en.wikipedia.org/wiki/Hastings_Naval_Ammunition_Depot,_Nebraska.

Russia, along with other Germans who were known as the Norka Germans.[10] To understand the Germans who migrated to America from Russia, I reference a date in history.

In 1763 Catherine II of Russia had promised the Germans who migrated from Germany to Russia that they would have free land to farm and that their sons would not be conscripted into the military service. After 100 years the manifesto was revoked, and my great grandfather, along with many of the Germans, migrated to the United States.

In 1942 the remaining Norka Germans were deported, and the German settlement vanished. The Norka Germans were not only refugees from Russia but also from Germany, so they had reason to experience fear during World War II.

My grandfather spoke German, and my father spoke Platt Deutsch[11] and English. It is today no secret that many German immigrants were the focus of discrimination in America during World War I.[12] My paternal grandfather's surname name was Brehm, as is mine.[13], [14]

---

10 "Norka," Steven H. Schreiber, last updated January 15, 2018, http://www.norkarussia.info/.

11 "Low German," Wikipedia, last edited January 17, 2018, https://en.wikipedia.org/wiki/Low_German.

12 "Anti-German Sentiment," Wikipedia, last edited January 12, 2018, https://en.wikipedia.org/wiki/Anti-German_sentiment.

13 "Conrad Brehm II," Tony and Cindy Lloyd, Find a Grave Memorial, last edited April 27, 2011, https://www.findagrave.com/cgi-bin/fg.cgi?page=gr&GRid=69013662.

14 "Brehm Line—Germans from Russia," Kathy LaPella, Geneaology.com, September 15, 2008, http://www.genealogy.com/forum/

I still remember the bomb explosion. However, not having experienced the intense fear of my ancestors, I can avoid: committing a self-fulfilling prophecy, and believing in apotropaic magic—an aphorism that intends to turn us away from misfortune.

"Will the chickens come home to roost?"

---

surnames/topics/brehm/458/; see number 215, VI, Conrad W. Brehm, my paternal grandfather.

CHAPTER 4

SON OF A BUTCHER

Slice of Beef

DO YOU WONDER why I look startled when I hear the "S-O-B" words? My dad was not only a poultry dealer but also a butcher.

In those days, a Nebraska butcher sometimes went to the farm to slaughter the animals, and my dad was no exception. At other times, my dad worked in a "Locker Plant,"[15] which is so named to this day.

I remember an extraordinary event when my dad butchered at a farmer's yard. I went to work with dad on a day when he was to butcher a pig. I was holding my

---

15 "Locker Plant," *Merriam-Webster Dictionary*, accessed January 20, 2018, https://www.merriam-webster.com/dictionary/locker%20plant.

dad's knives in my left hand, and I was holding my small Fox Terrier tucked under my right arm.

When my dad shot the pig, my pet dog tried to jump from under my arm. I quickly grabbed the little dog, thinking everything would be fine. However, in a few seconds, I felt my pants get wet, but I was not yet aware of the seriousness of the situation. What really scared me was the thought that I might have dropped his butcher knives.

"Hey!" My dad hollered at me as he grabbed his great big red handkerchief and quickly wrapped it around my arm to serve as a tourniquet.

I noticed blood squirting out of an artery of my right arm. I asked my dad immediately, "Will I die?"

"No, but we need to get mom to take you to the doctor."

It took about thirty minutes for my mom to pick me up. Dad showed me how to tighten the handkerchief around my arm and how to loosen it every few minutes

As the doctor was stitching the slash on my arm, he said to my mom,

"Say, this little boy doesn't even cry!"

I looked up from the table and said, "Would it hurt less if I cried?"

As a child, I was not aware how to express my feelings. I learned to ignore my feelings if they seemed negative. Today I have learned that the word *feeling* refers to the internal biochemical reactions to my sensory experiences.

My mind interprets these sensory experiences and perceives these bodily reactions as emotions.[16] Sometimes it may be difficult for me to express my emotions because of fear of rejection. At other times I may not be aware of the internal chemical reactions occurring.

My feelings are internal states, but I use overt behaviors to communicate emotions to others. Assertiveness[17] is the response I make to situations that validate my right to express my emotions without aggressively negating another person's right to express an emotional response.

I use the empty chair technique and re-enact a dialogue with my dad as follows: I sit on Chair Number 2 and I speak to Chair Number 1 imagining that dad is sitting on Chair Number 1.

Dad   Me
Chair Number 1   Chair Number 2

---

16 "Feeling," Wikipedia, last edited January 12, 2018, https://en.wikipedia.org/wiki/Feeling.

17 "Assertiveness," Wikipedia, last edited December 15, 2017, https://en.wikipedia.org/wiki/Assertiveness.

"Dad, I feel fear standing here waiting for you to shoot the pig. I would like to be further away. I will let you put the knives back in your leather knife holder."

I switch roles and sit on Chair Number 1, taking the position of my dad and speak to my imagined self, sitting on Chair Number 2.

"Sure, Robert. I just thought you might like to be a butcher someday."

I switch roles and sit in Chair Number 2 and speak to Chair Number 1, imagining my dad sitting on that chair.

"Oh! Thanks, dad, for the opportunity, but I would rather just be the son of a butcher."

CHAPTER 5

TORNADO ALLEY

"DAD, GIVE ME the candle so I can be the first to go down in the cellar."

"Robert, go down the stairs, sit on the bench, and hold the candle up so the rest of the family can see to join you."

"Thanks, dad, I like being the first one to look outside from within the dark cellar."

After having lived on a farm in Tornado Alley,[18] I was well prepared in accepting the inevitability of tornados.

I had learned to deal with stress. I have experienced earthquakes, volcanic eruptions, and hurricanes.

---

18 "Tornado Alley," Wikipedia, last edited November 17, 2017, https://en.wikipedia.org/wiki/Tornado_Alley.

However, I felt excited running to the cellar to escape a tornado.

We did not have a radio or television to warn us of ominous clouds or strong winds. Dad would go outside when the sky darkened to get a sense of whether we should head to our cellar. Dad would say the word "Tornado." All six of us would head to the cellar under the house.

On one such occasion, I remember that I held a candle in my hand and darted to the cellar, being the first one to take my place in the dark. I sat on a dirt bench, as I remember, and the rest of the family followed. We would wait as the storm passed by and then we would reappear unscathed from the tornado.

We still did not have electricity or running water. We burned coal for our cooking. We used candles or oil lanterns to provide light. Did I fear a tornado?

No. I thought it was rather exciting to run to the cellar and wait out the storm. When dad said, "Let's go!" We did.

I remember one event that was about as startling to me as the threat of a tornado. I was five years old when I learned suddenly we would be leaving the farm. I felt sad for a few days. I did not want to leave my pet dog, my pet pig, Tom the Turkey, or the other farm animals.

I could not change the fact that we were leaving the farm. I knew I could not avoid the fact that I was leaving the farm. Just as I had learned to experience going to the cellar to get away from the tornado, I had learned to view the change as okay.

At that time, I was not aware of the concept stress."
The term *stress* continues to plague research professionals with the lack of an agreed-upon operational definition.

On one end of the continuum, *stress*[19] often refers to an environmental condition that incurs damage upon almost everyone, such as a hurricane or tornado.

On the other end of the continuum *stress* refers to a person's ability to cope—that is, to manage internal demands or conflicts.

Somewhere in the middle of the continuum, the word *stress* refers to an individual's appraisal of a noxious environmental situation or to some sort of a complex interrelationship between an individual's learning to adapt to the environmental demand.

It is best to simply avoid[20] *stress* when I can, such as avoiding a tornado or hurricane. However, I cannot avoid *stress* all the time. Sometimes it's easier to change a situation. If that does not work, then accepting or adapting to the situation is likely the best approach, as the anonymous aphorism, "Accept what you can't change, change what you can't accept."

---

19 Cary L. Cooper, *Stress Research: Issues for the Eighties* (New York: Wiley, 1983), 81.

20 "Stress Management," Mayo Clinic, accessed January 20, 2018, https://www.mayoclinic.org/healthy-lifestyle/stress-management/in-depth/stress-relief/art-20044476.

CHAPTER 6

BIG FISH IN A LITTLE POND

Mom ASKED, "ROBERT why do you have tape on your mouth?"

I whimpered, "The teacher said I talked too much."

Mom replied, "I think you should follow the school rules, but you do not have to keep your mouth taped shut after school, do you?"

I remember one of my first days in kindergarten at Harvard, Nebraska.[21], [22] I was excited to go to school and to make many new friends. I enjoyed the rest breaks when I could eat some crackers and drink a glass of milk.

---

21 "Harvard, Nebraska," Wikipedia, last edited January 12, 2018, https://en.wikipedia.org/wiki/Harvard,_Nebraska.

22 "Harvard, Clay County," University of Nebraska–Lincoln, accessed January 20, 2018, http://www.casde.unl.edu/history/counties/clay/harvard/.

As best I can remember, I was sitting in our classroom talking out loud. Suddenly, Mrs. Rosebud told me to stop talking. She said that I talked too much. I was startled.

I did not yet know the rules as to when I could talk. She put black tape over of my mouth. I had the tape on my mouth the rest of the day of class. As I walked home after school, being the good kid that I was, I kept the tape on my mouth.

Sitting on Chair Number 2, I say to Chair Number 1, "Mrs. Rosebud, thank you for taping my mouth shut."

Mrs. Rosebud
Chair Number 1

Me
Chair Number 2

I reverse roles and sit on Chair Number 1, taking my projection of Mrs. Rosebud's position, and I speak the following to my imagined self who is sitting on Chair Number 2.

"Good, Robert. I hope I have taught you a lesson to not talk so much."

Finally, I reverse roles. I sit on Chair Number 2 and I speak to Mrs. Rosebud sitting on Chair Number 1. "Yes, I learned that you may tape my mouth shut for not following the school rules. I will raise my hand next time I wish to talk. I will not keep tape on my mouth after I leave school."

Harvard is a small town with a population of 916. Harvard is the 10,748 largest cities in America.[23] Think about it for a moment.

As a "big fish in a little pond," my entire class consisted of about twenty students. The entire school, K-12, consisted of not many more than 250 students.

As much as my dad had encouraged me to stand up to Tom the Turkey, my mom had supported me in stating that I should follow the rules at school. Mrs. Rosebud had put black tape over my mouth, and my classmates still supported me. They did not isolate or ridicule me.

I had coped with *stress* successfully before by running to the farmhouse cellar avoiding a tornado. Now, I had to learn how to avoid *stress* and adapt to Mrs. Rosebud's classroom rules.

Although I was initially startled from the enforcement of Mrs. Rosebud's rules, I eventually experienced *eustress*.[24] To wit, the high school honored me, along with my friend Max Keasling, as we were selected to participate in the coronation of homecoming queen.[25]

23 "Harvard, Nebraska, Population History, 1990–2016," Biggest US Cities, last updated October 3, 2017, https://www.biggestuscities.com/city/harvard-nebraska

24 https://www.merriam-webster.com/dictionary/eustress

25 https://en.wikipedia.org/wiki/Homecoming#Homecoming_Court

I did not know of the research on the concept of the "big fish in a little pond.[26] In a small school, if a peer group is supportive, does neither ridicule nor bully, it is easier to maintain a high self-concept. High self-concept is related to high self-esteem.[27] With a high self-esteem, it is easier to see oneself capable of adapting to school rules.[28]

---

26 "Big-Fish–Little-Pond Effect," Wikipedia, last edited November 17, 2017, https://en.wikipedia.org/wiki/Big-fish%E2%80%93little-pond_effect.

27 https://www.qub.ac.uk/sites/media/Media,366009, en.pdf

28 https://en.wikipedia.org/wiki/Self-esteem

CHAPTER 7

STICKS AND STONES

Sticks and stones will break my bones,
but words will never hurt me!

ONE DAY AS I was walking outside during recess, a kid called out to me, "Hey, Hair Brain! How are you doing today?"

I replied, "At least I have one."

Being one of the youngest kids in the school, I was not surprised that I might become the target of name-calling. My dad had taught me how to cope with Tom the Turkey. My mom taught me how to respond to teachers, so I had learned the rules of the game. Now I had to learn the lesson how to manage other kids in the school.

Coincidentally, in German the word for *mister* is *Herr,* and it is pronounced somewhat like *hair* in English. My surname "Brehm," does sound like the word *brain,* but with an *m* as the last letter of the word.

If I could re-enact the name-calling scenario today, I would use the empty chair technique. I would sit on Chair Number 1 and speak to Chair Number 2.

Older kid   Me
Chair Number 1   Chair Number 2

The older kid sitting on Chair Number 1 calls out, "Hey, Hair Brain! How are you doing today?"

I imagine I am sitting on Chair Number 2 and I reply, "Hey, I'm fine. Thanks, for asking. I'm new here at school, and I haven't met you before. Nice meeting you today, and I hope we greet each other again sometime."

As a five-year-old I had not yet experienced *bullying,* but I had already learned how not to play the role of *victim.*[29], [30]

29 "What Is Victim Consciousness?" Lynne Forrest, accessed January 20, 2018, https://www.lynneforrest.com/.
30 "Karpman Drama Triangle," Wikipedia, last edited January 8, 2018, https://en.wikipedia.org/wiki/Karpman_drama_triangle.

Today I understand the role of *bullying* and the role of the *victim*. For example, if I perceive myself in a *victim* role, I will always find someone who wittingly, or unwittingly, will play the role of *persecutor*. I have found that if I look for a *rescuer*, then I can find one. The horns of the dilemma--unless I learn how I perceive myself as a *victim*, I will not learn how to escape from the *victim* role.

In my role-playing example, I created the perception of myself as a friend, or *rescuer*, of my self-concept. I protected my self-concept by not interpreting my perception of the other person as a *persecutor*. Finally, I rescued myself by indicating that I perceived the person in a friendly way.

CHAPTER 8

GHOSTS OF THE PAST

I HAD ALWAYS cherished ghost stories,[31] whether it was the Tooth Fairy, Halloween, the Easter Bunny, Santa Claus, or the Holy Ghost.

We had just come home after having attended our church service. I always opened my gifts on Christmas Eve. I ran in the house, and to my surprise, I saw a shiny red bicycle.

"Who gave me this bicycle?"

Dad said that Santa Claus did. I asked dad how Santa got the bicycle in the house. Dad said Santa brought it down the chimney. I looked totally surprised. I went to look at the heater grate that led out from the chimney.

"Santa could not have come down this chimney with my bicycle."

---

31 "These 9 Hauntings in Nebraska Will Send Chills Down Your Spine," Delana, Only in Your State, October 10, 2015, http://www.onlyinyourstate.com/nebraska/nebraska-hauntings/.

Everyone laughed. I perked up and said in a tense voice. "Oh, you actually lied to me."

Were I to talk to my parents today, I would use the empty chair technique and speak to them.

I am sitting on Chair Number 2 and I speak to dad as I imagine him to be sitting on Chair Number 1.

Dad   Me
Chair Number 1   Chair Number 2

"Dad, you intended to teach me that Santa Claus was not just a literal, jolly old man with a white beard, dressed in red, who came around at Christmas. You and mom gave me the bicycle and were very kind, acting as the mythical Santa Claus I had believed actually was a real person until now."

I reverse roles, and I sit on Chair Number 2. I take the imagined position of what I think my dad would have said. I speak to my imagined self that is sitting on Chair Number 2. "Yes, Robert. Mom and I gave you the bicycle. We were showing our love to you."

Finally, I reverse roles and sit on Chair Number 2, and then I speak to Chair Number 1 upon which I imagine dad is sitting.

"Thanks dad and mom for that great gift."

I continue to be amused when I think how often I have dismissed stories as literal, having missed their figurative meaning. I am reminded of the following aphorism:

"All religions are true, but none are literal." Joseph Campbell

CHAPTER 9

BIG FROG IN A LITTLE POND

SINCE KINDERGARTEN, GETTING good grades has been easy for me. I found the eighth grade a bit challenging, however, as my mom was my math teacher.

After one of my math exams, I noticed there were two check marks on some of my wrong answers. As I remember it, I asked my mom to explain what the two check marks meant.

"Mom, why did you mark my wrong answers with two checks?"

Mom replied, "I was worried that other students and teachers would think I unfairly favored you."

"What? You mean you took twice as many points off my wrong answers? Mom, I do not like this kind of disfavored treatment."

It came as no surprise that year, except perhaps to my mom, I earned the valedictorian award.

As a thirteen-year-old I did not quite understand the concept of being a "big frog in a little pond."[32] I did not realize the relationship between high self-esteem and academic performance. It would be another ten years before I would be able to achieve high scholastic grades, as I had entered graduate school a "little frog in a big pond."

> Marsh and O'Mara demonstrated that academic self-concept among 10th graders was a better predictor of their educational attainments five years after high school graduation than their school grades, standardized test scores, intelligence, and socioeconomic status.[33]

I did realize, as I entered high school, that grades were no longer the most important priority for me. My focus changed to excelling in athletics, religion and music.

---

32 Chiungjung Huang, "Self-Concept and Academic Achievement: A Meta-Analysis of Longitudinal Relations," *Journal of School Psychology* 49, no. 5 (2011): 505–28.

33 "Big-Fish–Little-Pond Effect," Wikipedia, last edited November 17, 2017, https://en.wikipedia.org/wiki/Big-fish%E2%80%93little-pond_effect.

CHAPTER 10

ONE FLEW OVER THE CUCKOO'S NEST

Three geese in a flock.
One flew east, one flew west,
One flew over the cuckoo's nest.
O-U-T spells OUT,
Goose swoops down and plucks you out.

MY MATERNAL GRANDPA, Frank A. Wells,[34] was a lot of fun to be with. He taught me how to make great wooden slingshots. We took the twigs from trees and used leather strips cut from old shoes to make the sling. We then tied the rubber pieces from a tire inner tube to the twig.[35]

---

34 https://www.geni.com/people/Frank-Wells/6000000002005786736
35 "How to Make a Slingshot," Instructables, accessed January 20, 2018, http://www.instructables.com/id/How-to-Make-a-Slingshot-2/.

One day my Grandpa Frank surprised me when he said, "Robert, I will race you down the road."

"Okay, let's go!" Grandpa Frank darted out ahead of me, never to look back. He sprinted one hundred yards so fast that, for a minute, I thought I was standing still.

I saw my Grandpa Frank only a few more times in the next five years as, he "flew over the cuckoo's nest."

I was not aware of why, in 1954, grandpa was committed to the Green Gables Sanatorium[36] in Lincoln, Nebraska. Green Gables, which closed in 1956, could have been featured in the movie *One Flew over the Cuckoo's Nest.*

Months later I visited my Grandpa Frank at his home. He was mostly silent and was not like the fun and energetic grandpa that I had known.

In 1956 he was committed to Englewood Hospital in Hastings, Nebraska.[37] Grandpa Frank never returned home again. I visited him only a few times there. He died in 1958 after having spent his last four years in the hospital.

---

36 "Green Gables Sanitorium, Lincoln, Nebraska, 13 Aug 1916," Ancestry, accessed January 20, 2018, https://www.newspapers.com/clip/6795814/green_gables_sanitorium_lincoln/

37 "Ingleside, Nebraska, Home to an Early Mental Hospital," Jim McKee, *Lincoln Journal Star*, April 26, 2015, http://journalstar.com/news/local/jim-mckee-ingleside-nebraska-home-to-an-early-mental-hospital/article_2e7c28f8-17be-595e-9d5e-d5cf99e9fc3b.html.

I learned about electroshock[38] therapy applied to patients.[39] I saw the results of my grandpa's memory loss and listless behavior. I became keenly aware of the horrific treatment of the elderly.

It was not until my university years, however, that I realized how much influence my Grandpa Frank's hospital experience had on my choosing to become an educational psychologist, mental health counselor, and Psychodramatist.

---

38 "Electroconvulsive Therapy," Wikipedia, last edited January 19, 2018, https://en.wikipedia.org/wiki/Electroconvulsive_therapy.

39 "Hastings State Hospital, Nebraska," Asylum Projects, last edited November 22, 2017, http://www.asylumprojects.org/index.php?title=Hastings_State_Hospital_Nebraska.

CHAPTER 11

GOING TO THE GARDEN

In 1957 I was headed to the Madison Square Garden in New York. I had just been elected to represent the Harvard Methodist Church at the Garden. I remember the agreement with our pastor.

"Robert, you have been chosen to go to the Garden, but just promise me one thing--that you don't go up to the altar and become 'saved'."

I was surprised, but I said I would return to our church and deliver a sermonette to the congregation. By so doing, I imagined carrying the torch of my maternal great-grandfather, Charles Wesley Wells.

Great Grandpa Wells was the first itinerant Methodist Minister in the state of Nebraska. His book, "A Frontier Life," is listed as one of the "Forgotten Books"[10] that represents the hardships of the times and his reasons for converting the Indians to Christianity.[11] I entered Madison Square Garden[12] with thousands of Americans who witnessed the Rev. Billy Graham Crusades.[13], [14]

At sixteen, I was aware that I was following in my maternal great-grandfather's footsteps. My Grandpa Frank should have been the logical successor to follow in his father's footsteps. Instead, Grandpa Frank was a lay minister, but he was not successful in that capacity.

I received encouragement from my family and the church to dedicate my life to a religious calling. However, I did not experience any inner voice calling me to become a minister.

---

40 "A Frontier Life," Forgotten Books, accessed January 20, 2018, https://www.forgottenbooks.com/en/search?q=+A+Frontier+LIfe.

41 Charles Wesley Wells, *A Frontier Life* (Cincinnati: Jennings & Pye, 1902), 130.

42 "'57 Crusade Sparks Vision for Library Tours," Tiffany Jothen, Billy Graham Evangelistic Association, October 5, 2012, https://billygraham.org/story/57-crusade-sparks-vision-for-library-tours/.

43 "The Rev. Billy Graham," CBS News, accessed January 20, 2018, https://www.cbsnews.com/pictures/the-rev-billy-graham/6/.

44 "Billy Graham," Wikipedia, last edited January 14, 2018, https://en.wikipedia.org/wiki/Billy_Graham.

In fact, my experience with the Rev. Billy Graham Crusades increased my doubts about becoming a minister.

I was amazed how individuals would literally jump out of their seats and rush up to the podium to receive a blessing. Did I witness a religious awakening or a hypnotic trance?

I remembered my pastor's admonition that I should not rush up to the podium to be "saved" again. My thoughts that the Crusade was evangelism contradicted my belief that the ministry was proselytism.

I did not learn where my doubts would lead, however, until I enrolled in Nebraska Wesleyan University, where I encountered the full effect of my "cognitive dissonance."[45] I had serious doubts about religion.

---

45 "Cognitive Dissonance," Wikipedia, last edited January 19, 2018, https://en.wikipedia.org/wiki/Cognitive_dissonance.

CHAPTER 12

WHAT'S IN A NAME?

What's in a name? That which we call a rose
By any other name would smell as sweet.

WILLIAM SHAKESPEARE, *ROMEO AND JULIET*

"ROBERT, WHAT DO you have in your hand?"

I said that I thought it was a toy.

"Robert," my dad said very firmly, "Go back into the store and apologize to the storekeeper!"

I was crying, as my dad stated very harshly, "Robert, we Brehms pay for things!"

I apologized to the storekeeper and handed back a red coffee cup strainer.

And so, I had my first lesson in stealing. Not only dad tried to teach me the value of honesty, but the value of my name.

It was a dozen years before I had a conversation with dad about names.

"Dad, Superintendent Misston of Harvard High School, called me 'Brim' today." Dad did not respond.

I said again, "Dad, he called me 'Brim' --like a hat 'brim.' You're on the school board. Doesn't he know how to pronounce our surname correctly?"

Dad still did not answer. Somewhat exasperated, I said. "Okay, dad. I guess I'll change my name to 'Brim.' In fact, you can call me 'Bob Brim' from now on!"

I had been called Robert all through grade school and middle school. My name changes to 'Brim' was a conundrum. When I entered high school, I found that in high school I soon became known as "Bob." I felt proud that I had changed my given name and I vowed to keep my surname name "Brehm" as pronounced in German only when appropriate.

Although dad had tried to teach me how valuable my surname was, he did not dwell on the literal pronunciation. He intended to teach me that my surname, figuratively speaking, represented honor, but I was still into the literal interpretation of names.

I believed in the interpretation of names so strongly that I changed the pronunciation of my surname to "Brim." I thought the superintendent of schools did not pronounce my name correctly.

My sister told me recently, however, that my mom may have changed the pronunciation to "Brim," so that students could say the name easier. Perhaps dad also had changed the pronunciation to "Brim."

The joke was on me. I almost always pronounce my last name as "Brim." I changed my given name when I entered high school. I still use the name "Bob" with strangers, but I use the name "Robert" with family members. My surname is also very important to me. Were my dad alive today, I would share this poem with him.

Ode to my Dad

Remember the time, I wondered about the name,
Whether to say "Brim" or "Brehm."
Seems that it was not the pronunciation here,
But 'twas honor in the name you revere.

Guess you were just as puzzled as I,
And wondered how and why,
I thought the sound of the name was just a whim,
As to whether to say "Brehm" or "Brim."

Dad, I finally got the point, sound and clear,
You gave me my surname to honor, to revere.
Thanks for passing the name down to me your son,
In hopes I learned my lesson and not just for fun.

CHAPTER 13

BLOWING MY OWN HORN

"Hey, are you Bob Brehm?"

I looked down and quickly descended the eighteen-foot ladder as I was painting a farmer's barn during the summer vacation to make money for the up-coming college year. "Yes, what's up?"

I recognized Tom immediately as he was the most outstanding Nebraska college athlete in 1958. He said that he was prepared to offer me a basketball work scholarship to Hastings College.

"Thanks," I said. "I'll consider it." Ordinarily, I would have jumped at this opportunity, but something key stood in my way. The recruiter left shortly thereafter.

I recounted my outstanding year "blowing my horn." I received a superior rating at the district music contest for my trumpet solo, *Maid of the Mist*, rendered by Herbert Clarke.

The judges announced that I would play the trumpet solo, *Maid of the Mist,* again that evening. They judged my trumpet solo as Harvard's most outstanding music performance.

This was the final superior award that I received before graduation. I was also selected to play my trumpet solo, *O Holy City*, at my graduation ceremony.

Since I had excelled in playing the trumpet, my Hastings music teacher assumed I would be a music major at Hastings College.

I was elated in the anticipation of receiving a basketball scholarship.

Then I recounted my turbulent senior year of basketball at Harvard High.

We had just won the Class C district tournament. I had scored nine points, pushing us ahead. I fouled out, but my substitute was able to keep the opponent, Fairmont, from overtaking us.

I thought it was the best game that I had ever played, and I imagined that the recruiter was aware of that game. We had a 12–1 record in the regular season. We had lost only once to Saint Cecilia of Hastings. Their record was tied with ours. They had beaten us once on their home floor, and we had beaten them once on our home floor.

With our winning of the Class C tournament, we were scheduled to play Saint Cecilia again in the district tournament's semifinals.

The night of the semifinals will remain forever etched in my memory. We were ahead of Saint Cecilia. It was almost the half. Suddenly, the buzzer sounded. All the players were told to go back to their benches.

It was a few minutes until the announcer indicated that a medical emergency had occurred. A man in the audience had suffered a heart attack and died. It was the father of one of our players! The game was stopped, and we went immediately to our locker room.

Bowed in prayer, I was crying and struck with grief. My teammate had to leave the game. I was overwhelmed with emotion. I hoped the game would be postponed.

To my astonishment, the announcer indicated that the game would continue. I was ambivalent playing in the second half of the game. I felt sad that my team-mate's dad died, but I felt joy in anticipation of winning the game.

We lost the game by a few points, and I left in a grief-stricken moment. Saint Cecilia went on to win the final of the state Class C tournament.

We had a winning record of 12–2. Except for Alma with a record of 15–0, and Saint Cecilia with a record of

12–1. We were tied for the best winning record among all basketball classes, A, B, C, and D, in the State of Nebraska during the year 1958. I believed, had my teammate's dad not died during the district tournament's semifinal, we would have won. At seventeen years old, I rationalized our losing in the tournament's semifinal.

I did not know about the theory of "cognitive dissonance." When feelings or beliefs differ from our thoughts, then a "dissonance" occurs. To reduce "dissonance," we are highly motivated in changing our feelings to match our thoughts. It is predictably easier to change our thoughts. We rationalize to reduce this "dissonance."

I was excited because we were ahead in the game. I felt sad when I learned that my teammate's father died during the game. I experienced a "dissonance" between my feelings of sadness and my thoughts of winning the game. After having prayed in the locker room, it was easy to assume that losing the game was God's will. My thoughts of winning the game were not as motivating as my religious belief in grieving. Therefore, I rationalized losing the game.

I experienced "cognitive dissonance" again. Should I accept the scholarship and attend a Presbyterian college, or pursue my religious career at a Methodist college?

CHAPTER 14

THE HARVARD GRAD

"I GOT MY first degree from Harvard," I chuckled when someone asked me where I graduated.

"Oh!" came the reply.

Then I quickly added, "Harvard, Nebraska," and everyone laughed.

In anticipation of my second degree I said.

"Mom, I was offered a basketball work scholarship to Hastings College. However, since Hastings is a Presbyterian college I am driving to Lincoln tomorrow to enroll in a Methodist university.

Mom stared straight ahead. She was silent. My projection was that mom wanted me to go to Hastings College. My oldest sister graduated from Hastings College and remained deeply religious, much to the relief of my mother.

I surmised that mom's silence was an indication that I would follow in my two other sisters' footsteps who went to the University of Nebraska.

My second-oldest and third-oldest sisters had graduated from the University of Nebraska–Lincoln, and they did not espouse the Methodist religiosity

I had mixed feelings after high school graduation. I felt sadness for leaving my family, friends, and classmates. I felt joy for the anticipation of entering a university. I decided upon Nebraska Wesleyan University as it was a Methodist University and I could pursue my religious studies.

With the support of the minister of the Harvard Methodist Church, I rented a room in a private home.

I thought that I might also be able to continue playing basketball. As a "big fish in a little pond," I thought the adjustment to a smaller university would provide me with an opportunity to play basketball.

I remember my first day at basketball tryout in which I was preparing to compete for the positions on the court. I was shocked to find out that the regular coach was not going to work with the freshmen. Instead, to my dismay, an assistant who had played basketball at Harvard, and later at the University of Nebraska, was assigned to be our coach.

To make matters worse, I knew that my mom had taught him in her math class, and neither he nor my mom had good feelings toward each other. I felt some despair and reminded myself how mom had treated me when she graded me in mathematics class. I decided that

I could not subject myself to the assistant's probable subjective evaluation.

I committed the self-fulfilling prophecy that ended my basketball career. I made a false assumption that the assistant was biased, and then I jumped to a conclusion. I decided not to continue for the basketball tryouts. This was the beginning of the end of my university basketball endeavors.

I discovered that my freshman year was challenging. I was not prepared for the rigor of the academic study schedule. Unwittingly, I had no idea my first semester that I overburdened myself by taking German, Psychology, Philosophy, and English.

One day after class, my Philosophy professor approached me. "Bob, you are one of my best philosophy students. You would do very well as a philosophy professor in a university. I was surprised to learn that you are intending to become a minister in Nebraska. I don't think you would be successful as a minister, as most Nebraskans interpret the Bible literally.

Remember the Scopes trial as prosecuted by William Jennings Bryan whose statue stands at his house in Lincoln?"

I thought about the Scopes trial.[46] I realized how, even though staged, it pitted the "Modernists" against the "Fundamentalists;" so-called "Monkey Trial." Would I have to defend the word of God in the Bible over all

---

46 http://www.pbs.org/wgbh/evolution/library/08/2/l_082_01.html

human knowledge? Would I have to defend the literal story of the Virgin Mary?

I remembered the conversation that I had with my friend who had just completed one year of seminary at Yale. I asked him if he intended to become a minister and practice in Nebraska. I was shocked at his response. He stated very emphatically. "Robert, I am dropping out of Yale. I will not be a minister in Nebraska. Theology is quite philosophical. If you want to teach philosophy at a university, I do not see an employment opportunity, only a deployment opportunity. I'm registering as a conscientious objector."

"Are you kidding me John? What would you do that for?"

"Taking a position as a conscientious objector is very hard to defend in the United States. I would advise you to do likewise. I'm headed to Canada to escape the draft."

That was the last time I heard from my friend.

I did not want to escape to Canada or to register as a conscientious objector. My mind was made up though. I would transfer to the University of Nebraska the next year.

Mom and dad never discussed with me directly my transferring from Nebraska Wesleyan University to the University of Nebraska. However, my own projection made me think that dad and mom indicated their displeasure in my decision by withdrawing my membership

CHAPTER 16

GO BIG RED

Go Big Red!

I HEARD A football player suddenly shout, "Do you want a fight?"

I responded quickly, "Wait a minute!"

As a Cornhusker I was prepared for lightning, but less prepared for thunder. Before I could look around, I felt a hand pressing hard on my shirt collar, only to be held by a six-foot-four, 275-pound football player.

"These guys are NU dorm counselors, so knock it off!" Ever so grateful, I later thanked Joe for his efforts. Having played offensive defensive end at Harvard, I was no small fish here; I was six-foot-three and weighed two hundred pounds. Bob Lord, resident assistant (RA)[50] also appreciated Joe's efforts, as thunder had sights set on lightning.

---

50 "Resident Assistant Selection," University Housing, University of Nebraska–Lincoln, accessed January 20, 2018, https://housing.unl.edu/ra.

Bob Lord and I were on a committee to select one of football coach Bob Devaney's assistants to be an RA. We interviewed the candidate and recommended the now-legendary coach be hired and assist us with the college football players who were housed in Selleck Quadrangle.[51]

Sometime later the dean of student affairs called me to his office. He asked if I had ever thought of becoming a professional counselor, as he had noticed my interest and skill as an RA in dealing with student issues. He indicated that I could continue my RA responsibilities with a graduate assistantship and earn a master's degree in educational psychology.

Based on my three years' experience as an RA, and on the suggestion by the dean of students, I enrolled in graduate studies to obtain my educational psychology master's degree.

---

51 "Selleck Quadrangle," University Housing, University of Nebraska–Lincoln, accessed January 20, 2018, https://housing.unl.edu/selleck-quadrangle.

CHAPTER 17

A COMPLEX COORDINATOR

I am a complex coordinator.

"ROBERT, I THOUGHT you were pursuing a career in administration or counseling," said the former dean of student affairs, who was now vice chancellor at the University of Nebraska.

"Well, I just completed my masters. And I took a year off to teach foreign language, but I'd really like to go into the field of administration or counseling," I said.

"There's an administrative position with faculty rank as a complex coordinator at Oregon State University. If you took that position I think you could continue in administration or go into counseling."

"Thanks, I'll apply."

Just as I said that, I experienced "cognitive dissonance." My belief that I should become a counselor conflicted with my thoughts to continue a teaching career. I rationalized that I could resume my teaching career later if I wished.

Granted, I had been an RA for three years at the University of Nebraska. I had ample experience working with administration and with students. But I thought, what is a complex coordinator?

A complex coordinator was responsible for supervising four resident hall directors. The supervision included administrative decisions and implementing governing and discipline procedures for four dormitories housing 1500 students. The complex referred to the four resident halls that were joined together in the form of a square with an inner courtyard common to the dormitories. The complex coordinator reported directly to the assistant dean of students.

I accepted the position with faculty rank at Oregon State University for one year

I continued my postgraduate work in counseling psychology at the University of Oregon. Again, I experienced "cognitive dissonance." On one hand I thought I would like to become an administrator. On the other hand, I believed in the self-actualizing values associated with the field of professional counseling.

At the end of the contract year at Oregon State University, I decided to assess my options for the next year. I could remain as a complex coordinator at Oregon State University. I could accept a position at Clark College. An opportunity arose, when I read a flyer at the

University of Oregon. I noticed an interesting position at Clark College that combined all three of my career interests. Thus, I resolved the "cognitive dissonance," by combining all three interests into one career.

I was offered a position as assistant director of the evening program, counselor, and teacher of German. In retrospect, the new position at Clark College made my complex coordinator position seem simplex.

CHAPTER 18

THE FARM BOY AND THE LAUNDRY BOY

A diversity counselor?

THE COLLEGE PRESIDENT called me into his office. He began, "We are searching for a diversity counselor at Clark College. Because of your background, I wonder if you have any ideas?"[52]

"When I was studying at the University of Oregon I met a student who is eminently qualified. He is exceptional dealing with a diverse population, and he is graduating with a counselor's degree."

"Thanks," the president said. "I will see if we can make an offer to attract him. One last thing," he queried. "What is his nationality?"

---

52 Orlando Taylor, Cheryl Burgan Apprey, George Hill, Loretta McGrann, and Jianping Wang, "Diversifying the Faculty," *Peer Review* 12, no. 3 (2010), https://www.aacu.org/publications-research/periodicals/diversifying-faculty.

"American," I smiled and replied.

I was reminded of my own childhood and of the subtleties in name- calling. How do I pronounce my surname? Brehm, Braim, Brem, Breem, or Brim? Was I of German ancestry? Was I a third generation German? Was I half English and half German?

Thanks to knowing Kenny, however, I repeated, "American."

Kenny Lee and I met during my postgraduate studies at the University of Oregon.[53] We were enrolled in a course called "Group Dynamics," and our assignment for the Quarter was to interact in small groups. I remember that there were four of five in our group. Sometimes we chose to meet off campus.

As a class in group process we shared our stories with each other. I think this experience provided the foundation for my focus in counseling and in the importance of listening to the storyteller.

At the end of the Quarter, I reported our experiences to the professor. The group dynamic experience provided me the framework to understand each other on a human level. I transcended race and cultural ethnocentricity.

Kenny and I had much in common. Both of us came from working-class backgrounds. Both of us cherished freedom and education. Both of us were very idealistic

---

53 "Counseling Psychology," College of Education, University of Oregon, accessed January 20, 2018, https://education.uoregon.edu/program/counseling-psychology.

and independent. Both of us were the first generation to leave our homes in pursuit of a professional occupation. I was the third generation of German farmer immigrants; Kenny was the second generation of Chinese immigrants.[54]

Kenny Lee was not only the first diversity counselor at Clark College, but also was one of the first in the state of Washington. Kenny led the first group dynamics class in the state of Washington in 1966. He was a cofounder of the informal Washington State Community College Counselors Association (WC³). After Kenney's retirement from Clark College, he continued working as a multi-cultural consultant to education, government, and business.

---

54 "Chinese and German Immigrants," Carlee Swanson, Prezi, April 22, 2015, https://prezi.com/noa3sdraavpe/chinese-and-german-immigrants/.

CHAPTER 19

THE LITTLE COLLEGE
UP THE RIVER

What is the name of the college up the river?

"WHAT'S THE NAME of that college up the river?"

A short, portly man answered, "Green River College."[55]

"Oh," I replied. "I'm attending this convention in Las Vegas. Green River College is listing positions for counselors in Las Vegas?"

"Would you like to apply for a position?"

"No, I have a great counseling position at Clark College."

---

[55] "This Day at Green River, 1965: Openings for 100 More Students," Marketing and Communications, Green River College, June 2, 2015, http://grcc.greenriver.edu/about-us/campus-news/news/featured/?id=281.

"You should visit us sometime. We are in Las Vegas looking for the best and brightest counselors."

"Oh! You would not have to come all the way to Las Vegas, as Vancouver, Washington, is a lot closer."

We both chuckled and exchanged business cards.

Within several days after my return to Clark College, the dean of students at Green River College called me requesting information about my resumé. My experience included working on a Washington State committee that developed the norms for the General Development Test (GED).[56]

The following day I received a call from the dean of students at Green River College inviting me to visit the college. I agreed and said that I was most curious to see the campus of the little college up the river. The pictures that I had seen from the flyers at the Las Vegas convention depicted a very beautiful college surrounded by a forest.

After a short visit with the dean of students, he wondered if I was interested in a faculty position as counselor. He indicated that I could develop the job description for the position, and that I would be the counselor responsible for the GED testing program. I was delighted with such an offer, and I said to him jokingly, "Well, I will consider the offer, but I think I would work there just because the campus is so beautiful."

---

56 "Who Is Eligible to Pursue a GED?" Washington State Board of Education, accessed January 20, 2018, http://www.sbe.wa.gov/faq/ged.php#one.

We both chuckled. Within a few more days, however, the dean of students at Green River College offered me a very attractive salary with excellent retirement and health benefits. I did not know at that time of the exceptional opportunity afforded me creating and designing my counseling and teaching career at Green River College.[57]

---

57 "Summary of Professional and Educational Resume," Robert D. Brehm, Stress Guru, accessed January 20, 2018, http://www.stress-guru.com/Resume.htm.

Robert at five years old.

1942 Ford is a replica of mom's car.

Picture of a Nebraska road as mentioned in Chapter 1.

Old farm house where Robert was born in 1940.

Robert played in barnyard from 1940-1945.

Locker plant where dad was the butcher in 1945.

Harvard Football Queen

Crowned at ceremonies preceding the Harvard-Sutton game, Marilyn Evers ruled as the 18th football queen of Harvard high school. The king, who stands beside her ornate throne on the stage of the school auditorium, is football Captain Don Dunleavy. Janet Glantz, daughter of Mr. and Mrs. Ray Glantz, and Reicka Louise Koehler, daughter of Mr. and Mrs. Raymond Koehler, are train bearers. Robert Brehm, son of Mr. and Mrs. Dan Brehm, carries the pillow for the crown, and Max Keasling, son of Mr. and Mrs. Floyd Keasling, holds the queen's scepter. Attendants were Mary Lou Ballard, Wanda Lilly, Nadine Pauley, Lois Ann

Robert is pictured on right side of the Queen along with Max.

Robert in the university from 1958-1965

Study Gallary converted to the Human
Growth Center 1970-1990

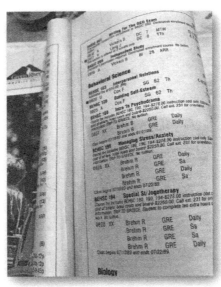

College schedule including Psychodrama 180, 190, 194.

Robert D. Brehm

Robert, the tall person pictured to left of center, received an award for having taught 45 years in the state of Washington.

CHAPTER 20

HERE COMES EVERYBODY[58]

AT FIRST, I did not receive significant support from students, faculty, administrators, and the community when I introduced the "encounter group" to Green River College. The encounter group focused on self-awareness, introspection, and interaction among group members.[59]

Skip volunteered.

"Now fall backward and we will catch you," I said.

"Wow, I could do this all day long," said Skip. Then Debbie, Linda, and Kathy volunteered.

The "Trust Circle" is often used as a first step in the introduction to the encounter group.

Debbie added, "I felt so much trust with everybody."

---

58 https://en.wikipedia.org/wiki/William_Schutz

59 https://www.amazon.com/SHARED-JOURNEY-Introduction-Encounter-OBanion/dp/B000OJ1OG6

Kathy continued, "Yes, I am amazed how much I seem to trust all of you. I had no difficulty letting go and catch me. Linda, what about you?"

"Well, I felt really trustful of everybody," said Linda.

We had just completed the first trust circle in our encounter group.[60]

And for the backstory.

When I was hired, the dean of students told me that I could write my own job description and design my program. I had taken him at his word.

I included in my job description the small classroom group experience. I wished that I would have had a small group experience when I was a college student. So, by including the small group experience in the curriculum, I could indirectly still benefit from this experience.

To encourage student participation, I negotiated with the student body and received the privilege of turning one of their "study galleries" into a group classroom.

Each encounter group was limited to twelve students. The encounter group activities are detailed in the book, titled, "Joy," authored by Will Schutz. [61]

To win faculty support, I requested that one faculty member from each department volunteer to participate in the encounter group.

To increase the trustees' support, I had encouraged them to participate in one of the encounter groups. I

---

60 https://en.wikipedia.org/wiki/T-groups

61 https://en.wikipedia.org/wiki/William_Schutz

was surprised and gratified when the chair of the board, revealed in a board meeting that he had participated with the students and me in a 24-hour encounter group. In addition, he strongly recommended that anyone who had questions about the group, should participate in the group.

He said he found the experience very enlightening and that the encounter group increased his self-awareness. He thought that he related much better with students, with his family, and with his business associates.

To win support at other universities, I invited a department chair from the University of Washington to participate in the encounter group. As a result, he placed some of his doctoral students in the encounter group. Since there was no encounter group experience at the University of Washington, this afforded a great opportunity for the doctoral student.

Subsequently, the encounter group experience evolved to an advanced therapy group. Green River College students took beginning, intermediate, and advanced Psychodrama. Not only was Psychodrama a premier therapy, but also offered college students transferable credit.

The Green River College department of counseling changed its name to the department of behavioral science to reflect its importance in conducting credited college therapy groups.

CHAPTER 21

RICK

Now you don't look like Gandalf.

"You remind me of Gandalf," said Rick.

"I do?" I replied.

Admittedly, I did not know exactly what he meant at the time.

As you may or may not know, Gandalf is a fictional character in *The Hobbit*, one of Tolkien's novels.

Rick did not elaborate, so it was left to my imagination, or introjection,[62] to understand which characteristics Rick attributed to me.

I did sport a beard at the time, so I did have a superficial resemblance.

I identified with Gandalf's attributes: wise, good spirited, encouraging, and supporting. Admittedly, I could be warm to students but just as sharp in speech. As

---

62 "Introjection," Wikipedia, last edited August 26, 2017, https://en.wikipedia.org/wiki/Introjection.

Gandalf, I had much energy to quickly criticize when I sensed wrongdoing.

Rick had been a business major at Green River College and decided to pursue his bachelor's degree at Evergreen State College. He received a paid internship at Western State Hospital.[63] It was during this time that Rick invited me to lead a Psychodrama[64] group with the hospital attendants.

Subsequently, as an experiment, and unbeknownst to the Green River College, I decided to arrange to have three hospital patients join my college class.

The objective was to determine if the college students observed any different characteristics between the hospital patients and themselves. I had not yet published a study noting personality characteristic differences between the interpersonal relation's class and the Green River College student population.[65]

At the end of the Quarter, the college students were asked to identify the three patients. The college students could not tell any difference between their personality characteristics and the hospital patients. In fact, the students did not actually believe that the patients came from the hospital population.

---

63 "Western State Hospital (Washington)," Wikipedia, last edited February 3, 2017, https://en.wikipedia.org/wiki/Western_State_Hospital_(Washington).
64 "Psychodrama," Wikipedia, last edited September 16, 2017, https://en.wikipedia.org/wiki/Psychodrama.
65 http://www.green-river.com/Research.htm

Because of their disbelief, I recommended that the college students attend the hospital setting to visit with the patients. The students were surprised that they could not tell any difference between themselves and the patients. They said they would never forget, before they had taken the class, they had stereotyped (MIO) mentally ill offenders.

I identified with the students. I remembered how I could not tell the difference between Grandpa Frank and other octogenarians, even though grandpa was treated as a mentally ill patient from 1954-1958.

CHAPTER 22

JACK

Welcome to the Dept. of Corrections.

"JACK, DO THE reinforcement principles that you learned in the group process class really work here?"

"Yes, I use both positive and negative reinforcement principles."

"You mean that you do not use punishment, only reinforcement principles?"[66]

I continued in my line of questioning thinking that I might find an exception.

"What do you do with the inmates if reinforcement principles do not work?"

Jack looked curiously at me, smiled, and said: "Punishment was/is always the default in corrections, but over the years, including my time at McNeil, I found how important incentives are to motivate people to not

---

66 "Reinforcement," Wikipedia, last edited January 14, 2018, https://en.wikipedia.org/wiki/Reinforcement.

get lost in the inherent depression and hyper-masculine environment that characterizes prisons. All people need hope, maybe prisoners more than most."

"Jack, I would like to bring my class to visit here."

"You can bring your class here sometime and visit with me."

"I would like that, as many students do not think that reinforcement principles work. In fact, many of the students who are parents think they need to punish their children to obtain good behavior."

Jack had taken the encounter group class in the 1970s. He was an excellent student, and he seemed representative of the college students of the times. Several years later I had the opportunity to have one of my classes visit the McNeil Island Correction Center.[67]

Jack was a most outstanding student from Green River College who worked with the prison population. He was promoted to the director of the McNeil Island Correction Center until his retirement. The governor asked him to come out of retirement to become the Washington State Department of Corrections Interim Secretary. Jack should be remembered as a progressive-minded-prison director who built national reputation, and even provided a model case opinion for the Supreme Court.

---

67 "McNeil Island," Wikipedia, last edited January 15, 2018, https://en.wikipedia.org/wiki/McNeil_Island.

CHAPTER 23

MARY

MARY SAID, "I always dreamed that I wanted to help young people."

"Well," I answered, "what's keeping you from doing that?

"Mary continued, "I will open up my own home and get started."

"Sounds good to me," I replied.

Mary had participated in the off-campus encounter group at Green River College. The group experience inspired her motivation to take action to serve the youth in the community. She invited some members of the group to "Braim-storm" (lol) with her about ideas that she had.

She owned a small house on Auburn Way near Main street in Auburn, Washington. Within a short time after she opened her home to youth assisting them in finding shelter, food, and clothing.

I served on the board of trustees of the formerly named, *Kent and Auburn Youth Agency*. The agency is presently named *Kent Youth and Family Services*.

At a board meeting when the agency bought the property in Kent, I asked the board members if they knew the history of the founding of the agency.

Silence permeated the room. It came as no surprise to me that no one knew of Mary's leadership role, as she was a very humble person. She did not want to take credit for her altruistic endeavor.

I am reminded of an aphorism that I think would have described Mary.

"I am not bothered by the fact that I am unknown. I am bothered when I do not know others."-- Confucius

CHAPTER 24

JERRY

I hear you should write a book.

"Bob Brehm," said Jerry. "Kreskin[68] says that you should write a book."

I replied, "Really?"

Jerry was in a Psychodrama group. He continued talking about the Psychodrama group experience. He thought it helped increase his self-awareness, and to cope more adequately with his emotions.

During the following summer, however, Jerry became combative with his family and he was committed involuntarily to a psychiatric hospital.

One day, following his commitment, I received a call from Jerry who was in treatment at the hospital. He

---

68 "About Kreskin," The Amazing Kreskin, accessed January 20, 2018, http://www.amazingkreskin.com/category/about-kreskin/,

requested that I speak with the therapists, as he indicated that I was the only counselor who had understood him.

Typical treatment in the hospital was administration of drugs, so I did not intervene to assist Jerry with Psychodrama during his stay in the hospital. After his release from Western State Hospital, Jerry visited me several times at Green River College.

For the next twenty-five years Jerry proceeded to write letters to me. The letters arrived at the college. I opened them. None of which I answered.

By my not responding, much as with the empty chair technique, the answers to the letters were left to Jerry's projection.

This was well before we had Facebook and Twitter. The new media allow persons, including hospital patients, to send messages anytime to anyone. The media allow, according to one's own imagination, that someone is listening and caring. Jerry was just a little ahead of his time.

As one of my therapy colleagues said to me one day, "You are vital to Jerry's survival."

"Yes, letter writing is therapeutic for Jerry."

CHAPTER 25

GEORGE

The owner will rent to George.

"You must first learn to cook an egg," I told George.

One might expect such a response from the son of a poultry dealer as I referenced myself in Chapter 3, or as the egghead that I am.

"I can do it if you show me," he replied.

"Okay," I said. "Let us meet on Saturday at the house your parents rented and cook an egg for breakfast."

George was so excited that he now had an opportunity to live on his own for the first time in his life. He learned to cook that egg for breakfast and was ready for the next challenge in learning to live independently.

A welding instructor at Green River College referred George to me for counseling and advising, as the instructor did not think that George would be successful in the welding program.

I learned from George that he lived in a Washington State adult family home. I visited his living arrangement, and then requested permission from the administration staff home and his parents to determine if George could live independently. I assisted George in learning to cook the basics.

In addition, for several months, I visited him frequently, acting as a liaison between his state supervisor and him. George was successful in his independent living and, I believe, obtained legal status as an emancipated minor. George accepted a position as custodian in the secondary school system after completing welding classes at Green River College.

According to the 1967 Washington Community College Act, Green River College was mandated to offer and provide comprehensive educational training and service programs for all citizens.

Subsequently, I received specialized training in Psychodrama from Dick Korn, and was certified as a Federal drug counselor.[69]

Many such students enrolled at Green River to obtain training, a high school diploma, or as part of a drug or rehabilitation treatment program.

---

69 "Richard R. Korn," *San Francisco Chronicle*, July 18, 2002, http://www.sfgate.com/bayarea/article/Richard-R-Korn-2794563.php.

In other words, the College served as an education and community mental health center that provided support services to all its citizens.

I was motivated to assist George. I identified with George in that I was a "big frog in a little pond," and I had to cope with similar challenges: learning to live independently, developing education and skills suited to my needs, dealing with disfavoring circumstances, and in reducing self-fulfilling prophecies.

CHAPTER 26

JOSE

"Hello!"

José had just called me from Florida. He had been employed as an air traffic controller, having graduated from the Green River College aviation program.

"Hello," I responded. "How are things going?"

"Funny you asked," he said. "I just got fired from my job."

"Oh! What happened?" I asked.

"They said that I have a speech impediment."

"José," I said, "you were assigned to Miami because you are bilingual."

José asked, "If I fly to Seattle, will you read the termination letter to help me see what to do?"

"Surely," I replied.

Within several days, José came to my office at Green River College. I read the termination notice to which he referred.

"José," I said, "I think this is an egregious mistake."

"Yes," José said. "I think I will sue them for discrimination."

And yes, José received a settlement. *Do you wonder why?*

Here is the story.

José was an immigrant from Columbia, South America. Within one year he had accumulated ninety quarter-hour credits leading to the Green River Associate in Applied Science Degree. What was unusual is that José took many courses by opting for the challenge. That is, he asked for and successfully passed the finals for many of the classes without attending.

José had completed his education before he immigrated to the US from Columbia, South America--in a seminary. It was no wonder to me that he was so well educated and bilingual.

First, what surprised me was that José was fluent in English and Spanish. Second, the Federal Aviation Administration (FAA) placed him in the Miami International Airport Control Tower precisely because he was fluent in Spanish.

How could the Federal Aviation Administration (FAA) have described his accent as an impediment?

I identified with "disfavored" treatment that served as my motivation to assist José. I was reminded that my mom had double checked my wrong answers on test scores. I was likewise reminded of my German heritage. I identified with José and his sensitivity to discrimination.

WILLIAM

I RECEIVED A call from a professor at the University of Puget Sound.

"I have a student here by the name of William. He says that you were his adviser at Green River College. He has a two-year degree, but his grade average is too low for him to be admitted at the University of Puget Sound. He told me to call you and that you would assist him."

"Yes," I replied. "Put him on the phone."

"Hello, William, what are you doing trying to register at the University of Puget Sound?"

"Well," William said. "You know that I want to be a preacher."

"Yes, but William, you do not need a four-year university degree to do that."

"Oh, I don't?"

"No, William, you can be ordained[70] and continue in your pastoral studies. You can also apply to be a lay preacher in your church's congregation. Let me know if you need further assistance."

The UPS professor thanked me and seemed surprised that I had solved the problem so quickly. And that is the last time I heard from William.

I remember his instructors at Green River College calling me and asking if I was his adviser. I said that I was. To my dismay, that did not usually seem to be a satisfactory answer. William was about to fail another class.

A psychology instructor called me and indicated that William was failing the class. I recommended another psychology class for William.

I told William I would be teaching psychology the next quarter, so it would be best if he took the class from me. William took my class the next quarter, and he failed.

I advised William to take the psychology with another instructor the next quarter. William passed the third time. I had assured William that taking a class again would not be considered a failure if he passed the course, no matter how many times he took it.

Whereas, it normally takes two years to complete an Associate Development Degree at Green River College; it took William six years.

---

70 https://www.wikihow.com/Become-a-Pastor

It was this kind of trial-and-error learning that eventually led to William's success in completing his Associate Development Degree.

I am reminded of my self-fulfilling prophecy when I did not even try out for basketball. I introjected that experience as failure. I admired William as he did not fail due to a self-fulfilling prophecy. By assisting William, I indirectly shared in his success and reminded myself how I had lost an opportunity before I even tried.

I had also pursued a career to become a minister. I identified with William as he did not experience "cognitive dissonance" in his decision making. I could now, indirectly, share with William's inner contentment in his decision making as I did with mine.

CHAPTER 28

TOM

TOM STATED, "I got laid off at Boeing. I'm enrolled in Green River College as part of a Boeing retraining program. While I am in retraining, my stint as a rodeo clown does not pay enough to support a family of five."

"Tom," I said, "if you had your fantasy, what vocation would you pursue?"

Tom replied that he wished to be an Episcopal priest. He laughed and stated, however, that it was a pipe dream.

"Tom, I urge you to contact your Episcopal diocese. You are very empathetic and perceptive. I think you would be a good fit for the priesthood."

Within a few weeks, Tom stated that he was delighted that he was offered a position as counselor at Saint Francis Boys Home.

Tom completed his two-year degree and then worked as a counselor at Saint Francis Boys Home in Kansas. He served as an Episcopal priest in Ellsworth, Kansas.

Tom requested my services as a consultant at both the Saint Francis Boys Home in Ellsworth, and in Lake Placid, New York. I conducted Psychodrama training groups for the staff.

I identified with Tom in that, had I chosen to become a Methodist minister, I would have been totally dedicated to the profession, as I am with counseling.

CHAPTER 29

DAN

"Brehm." I still hear an echo in my ear from the phone call.

"Yes, what's up?"

"Coach just informed me that I am not accepted at the University of Washington."

"No." I said. "Let me talk to the coach."

Sure enough, the coach said that Dan did not have his two-year degree, and he was not eligible for a basketball scholarship.

"Give me the person's name who stated that," I requested.

Dan had been accepted as a transfer student with a full, tuition-free basketball scholarship. But on first day of class he was denied admission.

I immediately placed a phone call and requested that the admissions office send me a written statement as to the reason for the denial of admission. I was informed that a committee would reconvene and let me know the reason.

That same day I was informed that Dan needed a college degree. I immediately called Dan and told him to come to Green River College the next day and fill out the application for an associate development degree.

The following day I informed the admissions officer that Green River College would send the proof of his degree eligibility to the UW. By the end of the day, I received a phone call and was informed that Dan had a nontransferable degree.

I asked the UW admissions office to send me a written letter that stated the college degree was unacceptable. The following day I received a phone call from the UW's admissions office indicating that Dan had been accepted.

He played basketball at Green River College and holds the record for scoring 50 points in one game. He broke his own record in another game by amassing 51 points. He was recruited by the University of Washington because of his excellent two-year community college basketball playing. He is the only basketball player in Green River College history who has received a full, tuition-free university basketball scholarship.

I was highly motivated to assist Dan. I was reminded of my self-fulfilling prophecy that ended my basketball career. Also, I identified with Dan's serendipitous surprise. Admission to the university and becoming a professional basketball player.

Most of my success in life, whether in receiving scholarships, awards, or in making career choices, also seemed surprising until I learned of the research of the "big frog in a little pond."

CHAPTER 30

SO WHAT IS THE REST OF THE STORY?

"Hey Merrily, I am surprised to see you here on campus.
Let me again congratulate on your honor of having received the *Green River College Distinguished Alumnus Award*. What are you doing on campus now? Don't you own a Montessori School?"

"Yes, my school is growing and is professionally very satisfying. However, I also like teaching art at Green River College."

"You have a natural talent as an artist. Your spontaneity and creativity would be also an advantage if you were training in Psychodrama."

"Psychodrama?"

"I just came back from Psychodrama training at the Moreno Academy in Beacon, New York.[71] "

"Why are you training to specialize in Psychodrama?"

"I prefer action techniques to talk therapy. Psychodrama utilizes role play to develop the spontaneity of the moment in creating a novel or adequate response to a situation. I will tell you more about it sometime."

As I walked away, I reflected on my interest in Psychodrama.

During my final year of graduate study in 1965 I read about J. L. Moreno and Psychodrama. My college professor thought that Moreno's ideas were too avant-garde, so our class did not learn about Psychodrama.

It was not until ten years later that I read Ira Greenberg's book, "Theory and Therapy." Ira Greenberg would soon be conducting a workshop at the Los Angeles Psychodrama Center.

I arrived at the workshop along with about 50 other attendees.

---

71 http://www.blatner.com/adam/pdirec/hist/stages.htm

I did not see Ira Greenberg at the podium. After about 30 minutes, some of the people began complaining about Ira's tardiness.

After another 15 minutes, I literally jumped out of my seat. I went to the podium and requested a volunteer to come up to the front of the room.

"I will direct a Psychodrama session while we are waiting for Ira Greenberg to appear. I have never directed a Psychodrama session, but I did read Ira Greenberg's book. While we are waiting for Ira Greenberg, I will start a session and then end it when he arrives.

I need a *protagonist*."

To my surprise, someone volunteered. For the next hour, I directed a Psychodrama session. Unbeknownst to me, a man had silently entered the room, sat in the back, and clapped loudly at the end of the Psychodrama session. That man was Ira Greenberg.

Ira came up to the front of the room. He apologized to the group for his lateness. He stated that he had been shopping for a coffee pot, so that we would have coffee break.

After the Psychodrama session, Ira met with me and recommended that I visit the Moreno Academy in Beacon, New York. He said Dr. J. L. Moreno wanted to train therapists who were naturally spontaneous and creative. In addition, Ira mentioned that he knew Dr. Dean Elefthery, who was a psychiatrist that had been selected by J. L. Moreno.

Ira recommended that I begin my training, by enrolling in a week-long training session in Psychodrama at the Moreno Academy.

In one of the sessions, Zerka Moreno, asked if anyone in the audience knew how to direct a Psychodrama session. I raised my hand. Zerka Moreno raised her voice. She wondered how I could know how to direct Psychodrama sessions when she said that she was still learning. She said that she liked that I had raised my hand, as she preferred Psychodrama directors to have confidence.

Following my attendance at the Moreno Academy, I continued my training with Dr. Dean Elefthery. I completed my certification with Dr. Elefthery and his co-trainer Doreen--two of the best Psychodrama trainers.

I was appreciative for the training sessions conducted internationally in Belgium, Switzerland, and Holland that provided me a multi-cultural therapeutic experience.

As I continued walking, I thought, I must share more about Psychodrama with Merrily the next time we meet.

ACKNOWLEDGMENTS

THE AUTHOR BENEFITED immensely in increasing his own self-awareness, and insight into the events described in this book and how they affected his life.

As to my language professors who taught me the value of learning the language and culture of my ancestors, I am forever indebted to my professors.

To my music teachers I appreciate the gift of teaching me to hear the song in each person's story.

I am most grateful to my wife, and to Green River College students whose stories I shared with the names changed to protect their privacy.

I am taking the opportunity to remind the reader, as I do students. The story always represents the storyteller.

ABOUT THE AUTHOR

ROBERT D. BREHM has an extensive in-depth background in counseling; as well as national certification as a Counselor, Psychodramatist, and state licensure as a Washington State Mental Health Counselor and state licensure as Marriage and Family Therapist.

In 1994 Mr. Brehm was the first in the nation to introduce to students credited online counseling courses with live streaming. His successful experiment with online live streaming from Green River College to a classroom in Mainz, Germany is noteworthy.

The encounter group thought to be the first college credited encounter group in the nation was the precursor to the some of the Behavioral Science Courses he originated: interpersonal relations, stress management, introduction to psychodrama, interpersonal growth for couples, jog-o-therapy, eliminating self-defeating behavior, and career exploration.

He also offered the first online live college course to a high school in a rural town in the State of Washington. The students were selected as high risk for graduation.

After completion of the course, all students graduated from high school and 50 percent of them enrolled in the university.

He has taught thousands of students in his career. His educational experience included teaching English, German, and Russian to high school and college students. In addition, he taught group counseling courses to graduate students at Eastern Washington University.

Robert D. Brehm was the recipient of an award bestowed on by the secretary of state for having taught 45 years in Washington State.

MY FAVORITES

"Homo sapiens are Homines
fabulatores."

—Robert Brehm

"Remember, when we're lost
in a story, we're not passively
reading about something that's
happening to someone else."

—Lisa Cron

"The more you leave out, the more
you highlight what you leave in."

—Henry Green

"The human species thinks in
metaphors and learns through stories."

—Mary Catherine Bateson

"That's what storytellers do. We restore order with imagination. We instill hope again and again."

—WALT DISNEY

"If there is a magic in story writing, and I am convinced there is, no one has ever been able to reduce it to a recipe that can be passed from one person to another."

—JOHN STEINBECK

"The story always represents the storyteller."

—ROBERT BREHM

"Life is but a mirror, in
whose reflection I see,
Not a myriad of others,
but a little bit of me.
To accept its beauty and perfection,
as if it all were true,
Must I not forget about
whom I'm speaking,
'Tis me, not you."

—ROBERT Brehm

Made in the USA
Columbia, SC
23 December 2018